CLOTHES MORE DEALS

The Art Of FRAMING POSSIBILITY

By Nathan Minnehan

A concise exercise in understanding how to re-frame the energies in our lives by designing the clothes we wear with the energy of success. One garment at a time.

If you Engineer the Feeling of Success in Your Clothes, you can Frame Any Possibility you Desire.

This book
with its valuable message
is presented to you by

____

CLOTHES MORE DEALS

The Art Of FRAMING POSSIBILITY

"The Secret to getting what you want begins
with Letting Go of and transforming
WHAT is holding you back."

-NM

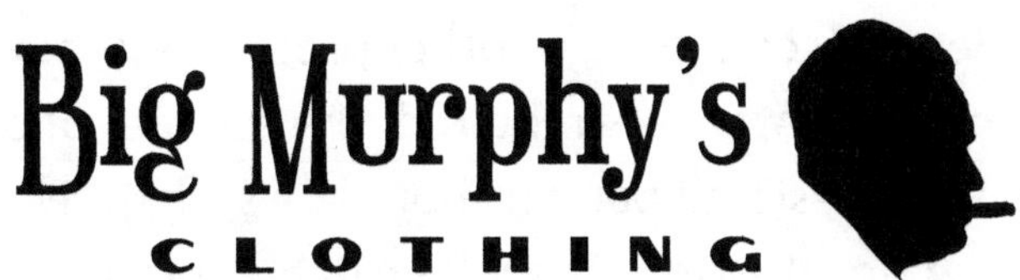

CLOTHES MORE DEALS
The Art Of Framing Possibility
By Nathan Minnehan

ISBN: 979-8-9949706-4-5

An Imprint of:

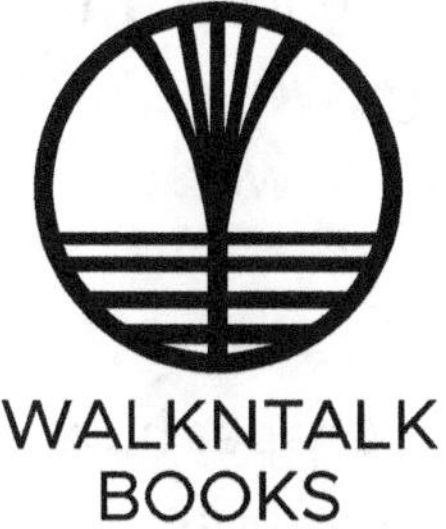

2336 SE Ocean Blvd #222

Stuart, Fl 34996

USA

"The Art Of FRAMING POSSIBILTY begins with what you put on each day!"

AAs the saying goes the best time to plant a tree was yesterday. The next best time to do so is TODAY. The garments that we wear shape the energy we live in, either giving us access to our powerful selves or worse denying that access.

When we begin to understand that how we feel shapes how we perform in every aspect of life, it becomes ever more interesting to consider the things that shape how we feel.

It becomes all the more important to engineer those feelings so that we can put them on each day as we go out into the world to BUILD OUR DREAMS...To CLOSE MORE DEALS.

A NOTE FROM THE AUTHOR

Have you ever walked out of your house before a big meeting, and thought to yourself, "Should I really be wearing this today"?

Or how about "Why the heck did I send my best suit to the dry cleaners when I knew I would need it for today! Today is my BIG day!"

Gone are the days when any of my clothes ever made me feel "less than," or heaven for bid I was unprepared for a special occasion. Over the course of the past 24 months I have invested Tens of Thousands of dollars into my wardrobe.

Today I live in a world where when I walk out of the house, I feel on top of the world, and I have the magnetism that gives me the super power to manifest my success effortlessly everyday.

Let me give you an example of my typical day...

Walking into Starbucks or my local favorite coffee shop, I hear a voice through my headphones. It's the barista.

"WOW, I love your suit!!"

"Oh, thank you, I actually designed it."

"What! Do you have a card?"

"Sure, I'd love to give you my card."

"Hey," insert here colleague's name, "he designed his suit!"

"What... that suit is amazing! And those shoes are FIRE!"
"Well, I actually designed those too. You can design your own pair on our website."
"CARD PLEASE," says the barista's colleague...

"Gladly," I say, handing him my card.

While you may be thinking, cool story Nathan, but are those people really going to be able to buy your suits?

Great question. Actually a fellow Starbucks lover and morning regular grew to notice me. We were introduced by one of the baristas. Because of our instant connection and my style credibility in the shop, I landed him as a client. His first purchase with me was $2500. He will most likely spend five to ten thousand per year with me building his repertoire.
So, you might be thinking. That's great advertisement if you sell suits, but I'm not in the suit business Nathan, how does building my closet affect my sales?

Well, so glad you should ask.
Jim Carrey says, "The most powerful currency we have is the affect we have on others."

What would be possible if in every networking event you attended, airplane you boarded, and PTA meeting you showed up presently for, you had with you a garment that in one simple way expressed you and your powerful life purpose objective in a way that allowed you to connect on a soulful level with a stranger within thirty to ninety seconds?

What if in your closet you had the power to cure depression, conquer your doubts, and soar like an eagle everyday?

Do you think you would CLOSE MORE DEALS?

You would certainly have the power to do so if you so chose to. Now, before we talk

garments, let's boil this all down to the nuts and bolts of transforming confidence and framing possibility with clothing.

GAME PLAN

What is the Secret to Powerfully Framing Possibility for the Obtainment of Anything You Desire?

Are you ready to live the life you have always dreamed of? To close the deals that will bring you the fruits to live your best life?

What if I told you all of this is possible so long as you are willing to let go of what is not helping you, and instead pick up the right things that will help you. The things that will bring you your success!

In this small booklet I will be giving you the tools necessary to open a new portal in your life, one that if you are willing to walk

through it, will transform everything you do into a success.

I will then show you how to craft moments that give YOU the Power, Brilliance, and Presence to CLOSE MORE DEALS in all aspects of life.

The bottom-line is if you are closing deals, then you are winning! It doesn't matter if the deals you are closing are business deals, social contracts, or any other situation you might find yourself in. It's about having that nitro switch to go Mach 3 and turbo your way to your next level at any given moment, and doing so effortlessly!

To build that switch let's begin by establishing a few ground rules for accessing this level of effortless strength and confidence.

CLEARLY UNDERSTANDING ENERGY

What is energy and how do we harness it for our benefit?

Mood creates energy. Energy creates mood. Whoever learns how to shape mood can shape energy, and charge the environment it touches with that energy. Does that make sense?

Imagine you've won a $100,000 interior decorating package for your new house. The decorator creates a mood board to demonstrate how she can make your house look and feel when you walk in. What type of feeling would you want people to feel when they'd walk into your home? Well, if you were married with kids you'd perhaps like people to feel loved, warm, and cozy. On the other hand if you were a bachelor single and ready to mingle, you'd want women to feel turned-on when they'd walk into your home. You'd want them to feel the presence of a strong, sexy man, while still feeling intrigued to discover what's behind the curtain. You'd want them to want you.

Now, on the other hand, imagine you chose to think decor didn't matter in your house. How then would your kids and family feel when they entered if you were married with kids? And how would your sexy, hot date feel if she were to enter your home? Would either feel safe, loved, or secure? Most likely none of the above, which brings us back to our first question.

WHAT IS ENERGY?

The answer is simple. Energy is what you feel. And what you feel is what you put out into the world. Therefore, if we can create what we feel by design, then we can have more control over our outcomes. We can build the framework we live, thrive, and succeed in ALL by design. We can win in life!

MOOD

What is mood and how do we create it?

Mood is the frame around the picture. Mood is what we see and feel first before we get the full picture. Mood is the vibe. Think about it. You don't say, "I got weird energy from that guy, there's a weird vibe there." You say, "I sense a weird vibe, that guy's energy must be whack!" Vibe is what we feel first, and energy is the full picture. If people don't like the vibe somewhere, they're definitely not going to stick around to test the energy.

Now, it's safe to say that mood is something we all know very well. We wake up in the morning and we sense we are in a certain mood. If you wake up alone you may feel elated to have your own space. If you wake up with the wrong person next to you, you may feel dread, and that mood may carry you into your day. So, what can we do to create the mood so that we can feel our best energy no matter who we wake up next to, and no matter what the weather looks like outside?

THE BUILDING BLOCKS OF MOOD

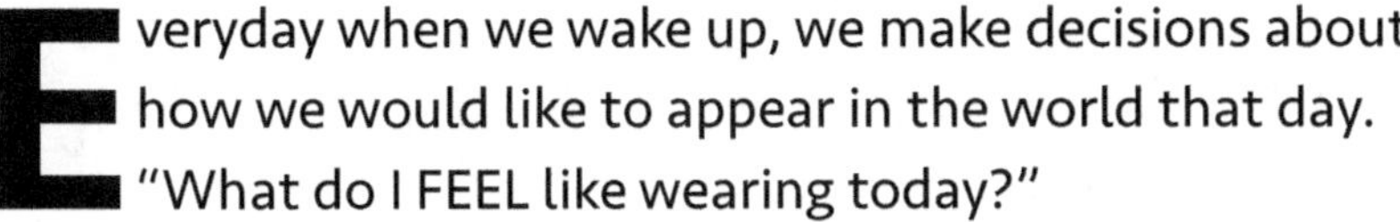

Everyday when we wake up, we make decisions about how we would like to appear in the world that day. "What do I FEEL like wearing today?"

That's right, in order to walk out the door you KNOW you MUST put on clothes! Unless of course you live in a nudist colony! However, I digress...

In 2019, when you walk out of the house you bring things with you. Some of the things you bring with you are things you wear, and other things are things that you carry.
What if I told you that the things you wear and carry are carrying you? That the mood they create crafts the energy you live in that day, and if done on purpose can make you powerful beyond measure.
By default, if you put on clothes that don't make you feel powerful, that depress you deep down, that make you feel less confident, then you are accepting a frame that makes you feel 'less than'. As a result, you will be putting an energy of "less than" into the world.

From the Science of Getting Rich by Wallace Wattles, we learn that the most important feelings to feel are "gratitude" and “increase”. No matter what, if you can feel gratitude everyday for the life you’ve been given and act in such a way as to portray increase, you WILL create the future you desire!

RE-THINKING THE WAY WE WAKE UP

What would it look like if everyday you woke up and read something that DEFINITELY reminded you of where you were going in life? Then, what if you put something on that made you feel like you were already there? Then, what if you walked out the door and executed every day powerfully moving through the world with that energy? With that statement about your purpose and direction in life, you would be living on purpose with the energy of success!

Now, what would your life look like? How would people say hello to you? How would your conversations with colleagues, customers, and clients be different? Who would be leading the conversation, you or them?

How would they hear you differently? How would they see you differently? How would this shift speed up your success, and ultimately help you close more deals?

YOU ARE NOT YOUR CLOTHES BUT YOUR CLOTHES CRAFT YOUR ENERGY SO YOU CHOOSE

Many moons ago I was walking to school when a classmate joined me and I noticed his exquisite jacket, pants, and boots. Even his backpack was mint. I commented on his style. "The clothes make the man," he said. That moment stuck with me. It was something I battled, not believing that materials could create the individual. However as I got older and began building a wardrobe I noticed myself shopping on price, going to second hand, buying suits from my Turkish tailor, and shirts he "custom made", even though they weren't measured for me! I sought out suits online for cheap, and even convinced myself I looked great in my grandfather's old suits I had altered. This paradigm eventually bankrupted itself the day I met my mentor. He walked into the room and time stopped. His energy, smile, and presence were larger than life. He was a sartorial savant, and I was intrigued. When I found out the price of his jacket I nearly fell over. I had no idea things could be so expensive. He quickly educated me.

"If you want to close real deals, and do real business, you have to dress with the correct materials."

"Clothes are not expensive, clothes create the close and that's profit! It's the other way around!"

We walked to his store and I tried on my first investment piece. I had never felt that feeling. That power. That material. Suddenly I looked at everything else I was wearing and soon it all felt like a leaky ship. Feeling the power of that garment revealed energy gaps in the clothes I was already wearing. The next few years were massively transformative. I looked at my closet and realized that the guy getting dressed everyday was sabotaging my real success. I looked in the mirror and realized something had to change. I began to look forward to crafting more garments. I sorted my clothing into two groups. I realized I had been buying clothing that was interesting, however there was little to no continuity between the garments. I thought I had built a wardrobe, when really I had collected a closet that resembled a compost of garments I hardly wore, and yet I wondered why I wasn't getting the results I wanted in my life.

CREATE AND DESTROY

One of my most influential life mentors, Dr. Gene Landrum, the creator and founder of Chuck E. Cheese, once said "you have to be willing to intentionally destroy yourself in order to powerfully re-create yourself." What he meant by this was that you have to be willing to let go in order to receive. If you make space for the new you can receive the new you. If you're stubborn and unwilling to admit that the things you are doing are not working, then how can you change them? The most powerful tool we have is change, and yet the whole world resists it. What would it take for this message to really sink in? What would it take for you to make the change you know you desperately need to make in your life?

THE EXPERIMENT

Consider Donating All of your Clothes

How much of your closet do you really wear? Five to ten shirts? Five to ten suits? A few casual slacks? Ten to fifteen pair of underwear, and twenty socks and plain white or black tees? A couple of dress shoes? One or two pair of sneakers?

What would your life look like if the clothes you wore made you feel, embody, and attract your success everyday? What if you could rid your life of all of your previous inhibitions? What if you could reconstruct the real, powerful you through clothing that told the story about your commitment to success, and your life purpose? What if the vibration of your unique vision of success was designed into your clothing like a chip into a computer to run the program of success everyday?

Then what would be possible?

EFFORTLESSLY MANIFESTING YOUR SUCCES

WHAT IS YOUR Narrative and what does it have to do with your success?
"The Story You're Telling Yourself and The World Around You Without Saying a Word." – Narrative

When you wake up in the morning and get dressed, you put on stories. Those stories then walk out the door with you and speak singlehandedly. The way those clothes are making you feel is either putting out a contagious vibe of success, or detracting from success by making you subconscious and feel "less than".

What is it then costing you not to look and feel your best everyday? How is your half-baked wardrobe serving your self-conscious need to sabotage yourself for fear that you might outshine or offend others along the way?

What would it take to give yourself permission to take back your right to live fully empowered, and make a real investment in yourself?

ACCESSING POSSIBILITY THROUGH CLOTHING

If you're still reading this, then you're most likely beginning to see the point. You are beginning to realize that how you feel is very important. How you feel affects how you perform, and how others see you. What if we were to flip the script? Instead of asking why someone would invest in their wardrobe, and spend real money on clothing, ask instead, why wouldn't someone powerfully moving in the direction of their success, invest in themselves by investing in their clothing? Which brings us to the next point.

PERSONAL BRAND —> BUILD IT OR KILL IT!

In the community of people you operate in, both online and in person, you have a certain type of perception you have crafted about yourself. People either talk about you or they don't. They either love you, hate you, or Worse, Don't Even Notice you!

What is your personal brand, and how do you create it?

Your personal brand begins with that energy you bring into the world. The way you make others feel! It's what you do, how you do it, and what you're known for. When it comes to clothing and building a wardrobe, I have successfully helped powerful people around the globe enhance their personal brands by crafting garments for them that tell stories that instantly confer their value, influence, and brilliance on the world around them.

From Dr. Greg Reid, author of 65 books and counting, to Kajabi co-founder, Travis Rosser, to the creator of the Make A Wish foundation, Frank Shankwitz, to Ron Klein, the inventor of the magnetic strip on the credit card, and several other famous people living their best lives, I have had the pleasure of helping all of them tell powerful stories with their garments.

When a jacket, suit, shirt, or coat you are wearing has been designed for you it carries with it an energy more powerful than the most expensive GUCCI or Prada piece off the rack.

PEOPLE WILL NOTICE AND OFTEN ASK.

EXAMPLE 1 [Exercising the "CLOSE" / CLOTHES]

"Wow that's a beautiful jacket, I love the stitching."

ANSWER:
"Oh thank you, this is my clarity jacket. The blue stitching is one of my mantras for success and clarity in everything I do."

"Really? Tell me more about that, what do you do?"
"Well, I help real people find real value in their next real estate purchase."
"Wow, that's powerful, my husband and I were just thinking about buying an investment property here in the Fort Lauderdale area. Our daughters just moved down here for college."

"Oh really," he says opening his jacket. "I keep my kids right here with me everyday. They're the motivation behind everything I do, and so I have photos of them in the lining of all of my suits and jackets."

"GET OUT OF HERE!" "Wow, that is so powerful. My husband and I are definitely going to call you!"

"Here, would you mind punching in your best contact information? I'll send you a text with my info."

"Oh perfect, yes, that's easy. Great, well thank you so much! My husband and I will most definitely be in touch!"

"Thank you miss. I will send you my information now."

"Okay great, take care!"

Observations

Did you notice how the man's jacket instantly gave him control in the conversation? How everything they were talking about went directly back to what he was wearing, almost like flaps in a pinball machine? He kept wracking up the points, over and over until she reached a point of certainty that she will definitely reach out. Then, the trained "closer," not wanting to leave anything up to chance made the smartest next move, and gave her his phone with an open contact allowing her to easily give him the best contact information. With all of the balls now in his court, it's up to him to score.

PERSONAL BRAND RESIDUALS

What Other People Say about You Is a Residual you Can create through the Power of Your Personal Brand!

The other day I received a phone call.

"Hello, this is Nathan."

"Yes, Nathan, this is Mark."

"Hi Mark, how can I help you?"

"Well, I need help with my website and Jackie told me she knows the only guy to work with and gave me your information. I looked you up online, saw your suits and instantly I knew you were the guy!"

"Well, thank you Mark. What kind of project, timeline, and budget are we working with here?"

"I have six hundred shoes to move before Christmas. I need a new e-commerce store in two weeks, and I want to pump Instagram with ads to sell out all of my shoes!"

"Excellent! You're talking to the guy who can make that happen. What do you say I take a look at your product, and get you a quote in forty-eight hours and we'll move forward then? Does that sound good?"

"Yes! I just love your style, and professionalism, and I know you're the guy for the job!"

"Excellent, thank you Mark. I will call you Thursday at this same time. Does that work for you?"
"Yes that's perfect, thank you Nathan!"
"It's my pleasure Mark. I look forward to positioning your brand for success!"

"Okay, talk soon."

"Bye now."

How likely do you think Mark is to buy from Nathan? Why was Mark referred to Nathan? What did Nathan do to become the guy who owns a suit company, yet has created a personal brand that establishes trust with perfect strangers to do business with him on a completely different vertical?

Simple Answer: He invested in himself and spent real time, real money, and real energy building his wardrobe and online image.

Longer Answer:

Nathan took the advice of Dr. Gene Landrum and intentionally destroyed himself to powerfully re-create himself. He donated/ gifted nearly all most of his clothes and rebuilt his wardrobe one intentional garment at a time. He established a mantra that frames every garment he wears and therefore sets the mood of success so that he feels the energy of success everyday, everywhere he goes. Anything in his closet that made him feel "less than" he donated or gifted. He designed clothing that told stories to himself and others that established confidence and trust in himself and his abilities.

What else did he do to earn that reputation?

He moved. He gave up the old apartment that was holding him back. He moved into a new energy by crafting a new frame. He donated his clothes, built every new garment by design, and let go of a house and a city that no longer defined him. He changed his energy, and therefore changed his life. He examined all of the ways he was appearing online and reached his next level of success by intentionally destroying to powerfully recreate himself. He hired photographers and branding gurus to help him reach his next level, and vowed to never be complacent.

CLOSING THOUGHTS

If you're not growing you're shrinking. If you're not living, you're dying.

"An old suit carries with it old inhibitions, a new suit carries with it a blank canvas, and the possibility of a new powerful version of oneself" -Prentice Mulford, Thoughts are Things

Put simply, if any of the garments in your closet remind you of your failures or previous inhibited states, then they need to go.

It's time to do some math and decide how much you can afford to spend on

your wardrobe yearly, then double that figure. "Double it?" Yes, "double it."

Garments created just for you as illustrated in the previous stories will not cost you money. They will MAKE YOU MONEY. They will help you CLOSE MORE DEALS.

TAKE ACTION

To find out more about how you can begin to CLOSE MORE DEALS, reach out to one of Nathan's team members and schedule your first truly bespoke success clothing consultation with the man writing this text!

IF you want success, then you must engineer it. Begin first by engineering the mindset, setting the mood, tone, vibe, and energy of success with garments that convert more situations in your life into the success you desire. The success that gives you the WIN!

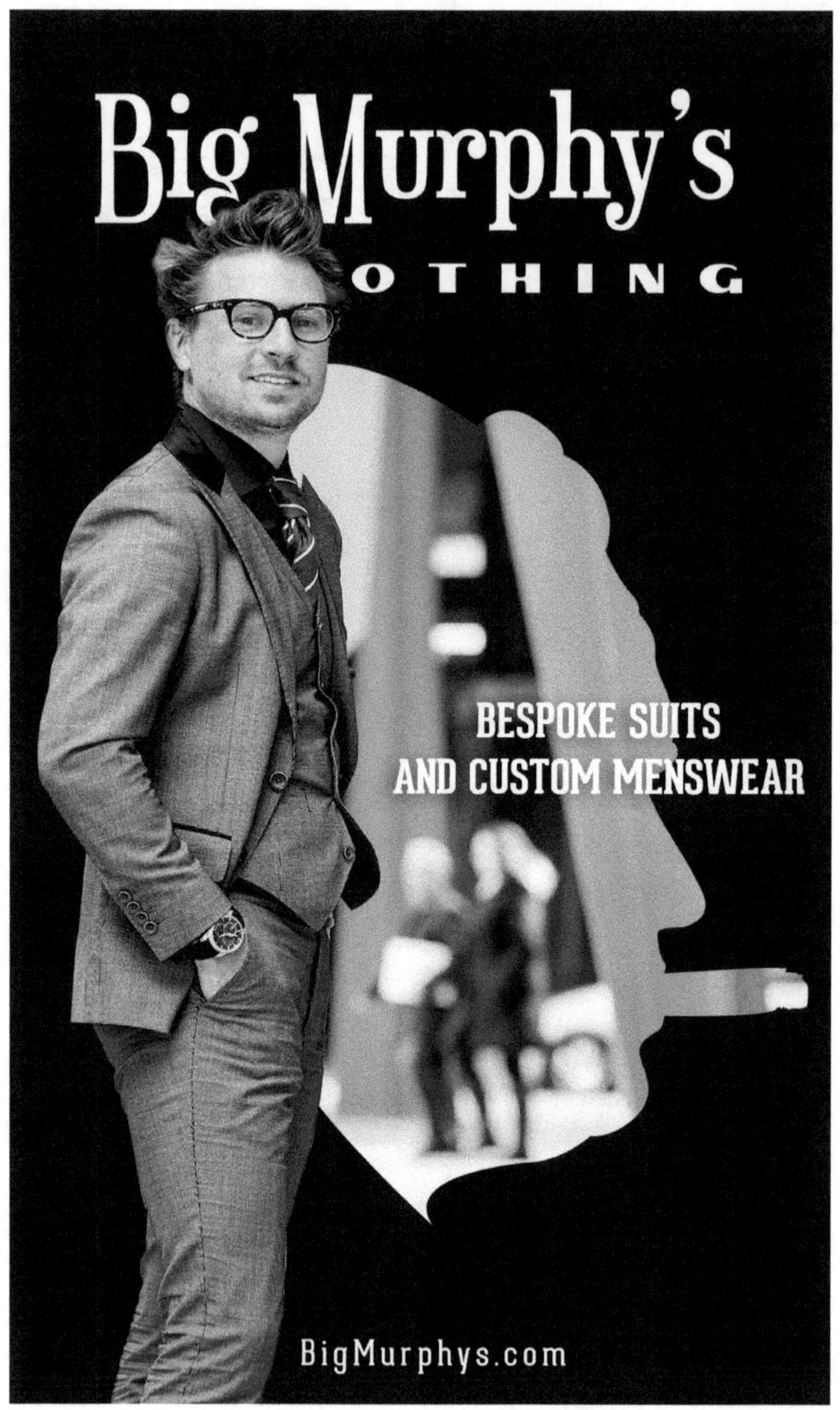
Big Murphy's
OTHING
BESPOKE SUITS
AND CUSTOM MENSWEAR
BigMurphys.com

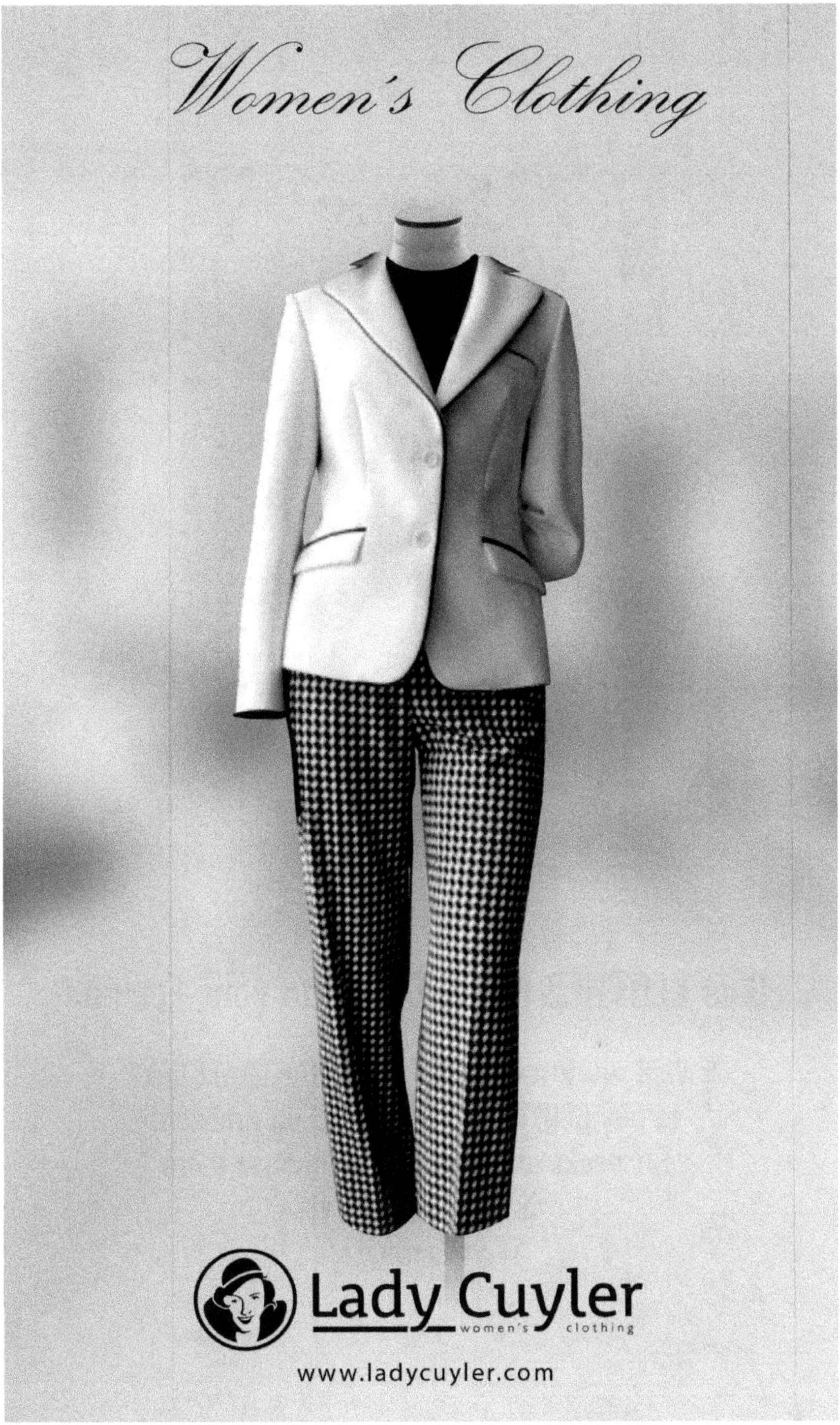

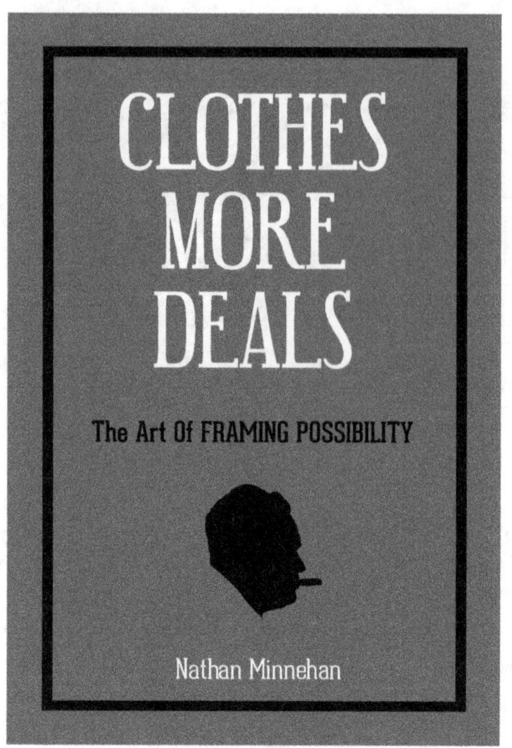

Give CLOTHES MORE DEALS to your Friends

Visit www.nathan.life to find the direct link
to buy CLOTHES MORE DEALS on Amazon.
For packs of 100 you can purchase them
directly from us via:
www.nathan.life

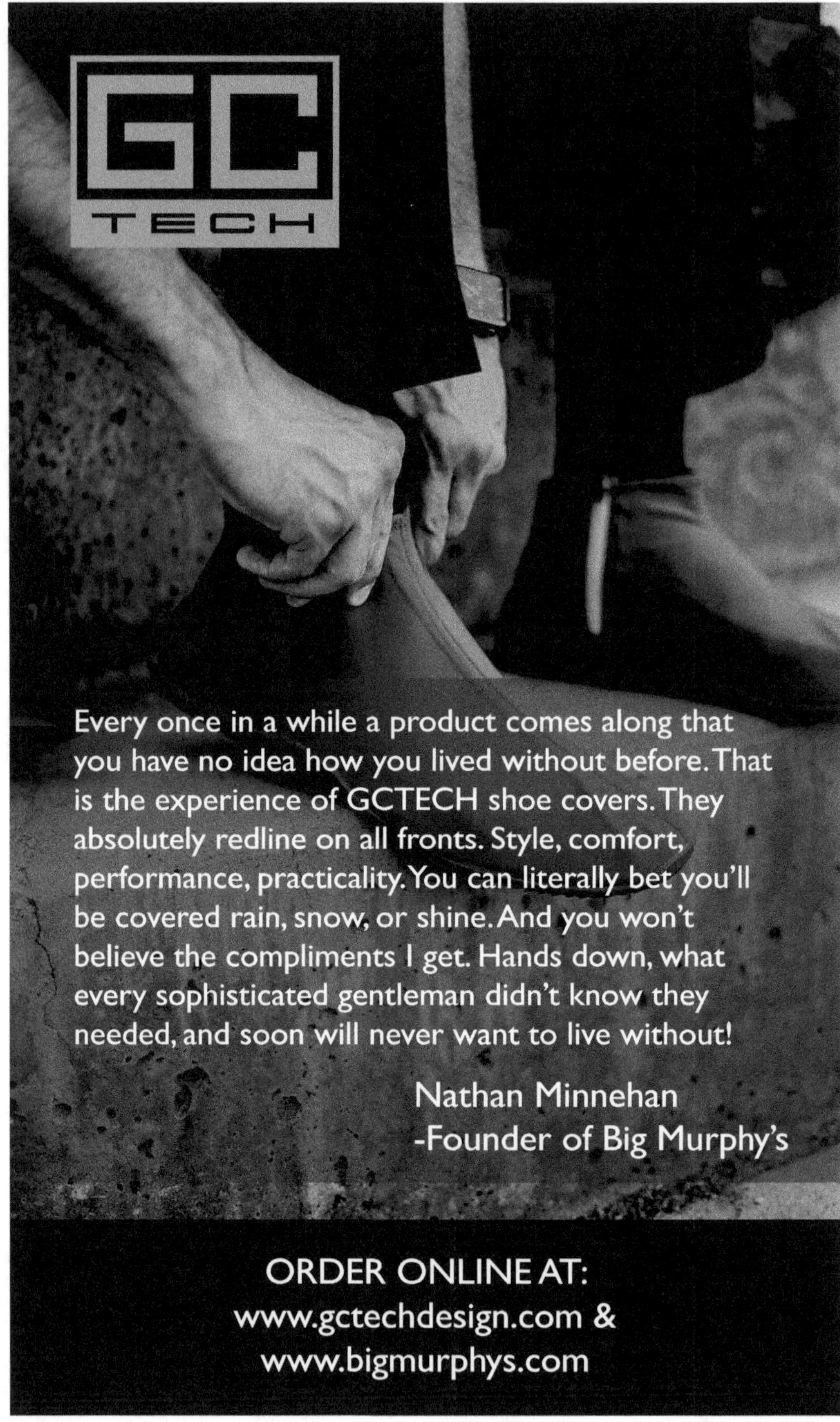
GC
TECH
Every once in a while a product comes along that you have no idea how you lived without before. That is the experience of GCTECH shoe covers. They absolutely redline on all fronts. Style, comfort, performance, practicality. You can literally bet you'll be covered rain, snow, or shine. And you won't believe the compliments I get. Hands down, what every sophisticated gentleman didn't know they needed, and soon will never want to live without!
Nathan Minnehan
-Founder of Big Murphy's
ORDER ONLINE AT:
www.gctechdesign.com &
www.bigmurphys.com

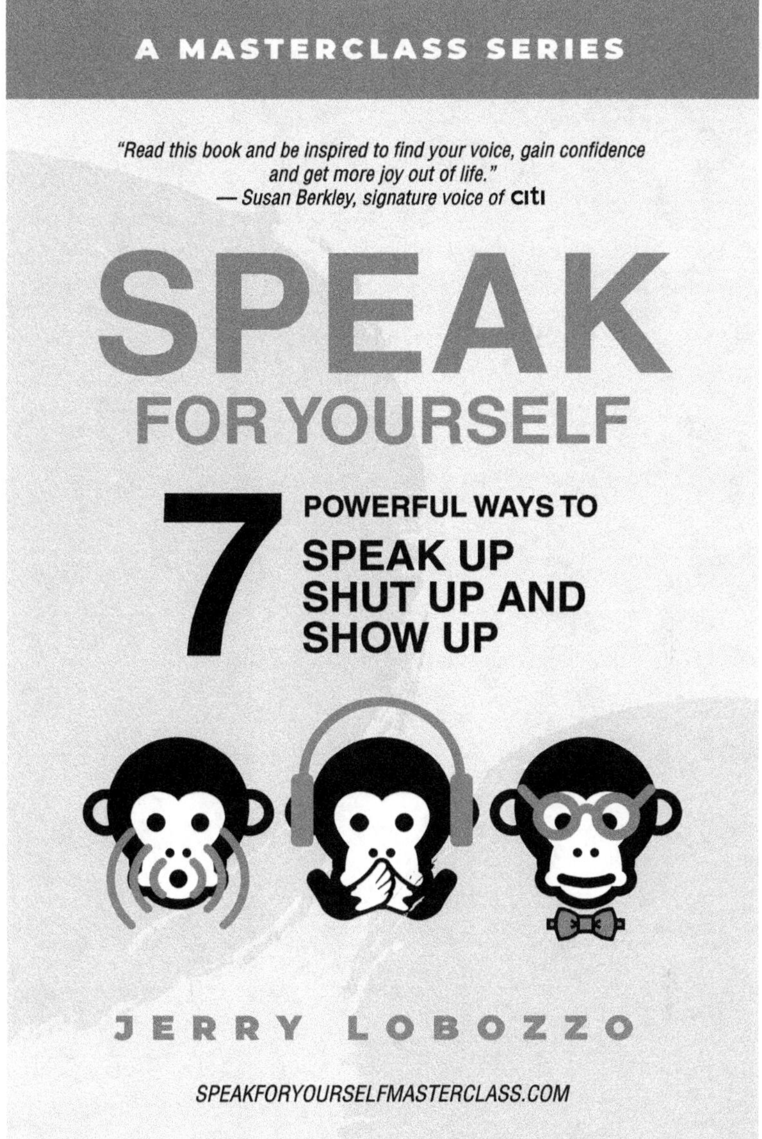

Oh, by the way, do yourself a favor, and get this book!

www.ingramcontent.com/pod-product-compliance
Lightning Source LLC
LaVergne TN
LVHW010945110826
845149LV00013B/2766

* 9 7 9 8 9 9 4 9 7 0 6 4 5 *